The Prayer Journal Secrets of an Intercessor

Jonathan McGee

DEDICATION

This Book is Dedicated to my Prayer Warrior Mother Ethyl McGee who taught me how to pray the word of God in all Situations for which I am a result, Reverend Pearl Jackson who taught me the power of Praying in the Spirit, Apostle A. A Perez the first man who taught me men need to be intercessors, also my siblings Krystin, Khloe, Krystina, and AJ who were my first assignments in Prayer.

Jonathan McGee

CONTENTS

FOREWARD

Have you ever noticed that one of the least attended meetings in some churches are intercessory prayer meetings?

Having pastored for 30 years, I now realize that many did not attend because they felt prayer and intercession was not that important. They also felt that their prayers were not being answered and others didn't really see a need to even attend.

Even as a child growing up the real meaning of prayer and intercession was not emphasized as a result of having a relationship and intimate fellowship with God as your Father. Prayer is releasing the heart and will of God into the earth.

Prayer and intercession are subjects that are misunderstood and undervalued by many in the body of Christ. In the 'Journal of An Intercessor", you will learn that prayer and intercession is not something that we do as a ritual or duty. Prayer and intercession is not to be a script, or a bell hop to get what we want when we have a need or a problem. Prayer and intercession is the track that allows heaven to flow into earth.

In *'Journal of An Intercessor'*, Jonathan not only teaches on the purpose of prayer and intercession, but he allows you into his prayer time and demonstrates what real prayer and intercession looks like. Having experienced the good, bad and ugly tests and trials in his life, he has learned a level of prayer and intercession that God is allowing him to share with the body of Christ. Jonathan brings soundness and stability where there has been foolishness and flakiness in the body Christ. His love and fervency for prayer and intercession is truly expressed in his life and his writings.

As a young intercessor, he writes from a place of knowing the Father as a Son and how to be led by the Holy Spirit. The *'Journal of An Intercessor'* is for those who are being moved by the Spirit to go deeper in prayer and intercession but lacked knowledge. I believe this book is the first of many that will help others hear and see in the Spirit realm to release God's will for their life and the lives of those they are called to intercede for. As a spiritual son, Jonathan has proven his ability to set the captives free through prayer and intercession, as well as preaching the word of God.

If you are hungry for more of God or need a catalyst to go deeper in intercession, then let this be the beginning of your journey into your journal as an intercessor and prayer warrior.

I also highly recommend this book for prayer ministries and prayer groups as a study guide and tool for developing personal prayer and intercession.

Dorrine Jones
Founder, School of The Woman
Dorrine Jones Ministry

Jonathan McGee

1 AFTER THIS MANNER

Matthew 6:6 (AMPC)

But when you pray, go into your [most] private room, and, closing the door, pray to your Father, who is in secret; and your Father, who sees in secret, will reward you in the open.

What is prayer? How do I pray? How to I expand my prayer life? All of these questions will be answered within the pages of this book. Prayer may be a conversation between you and the Father, however that is not all that prayer is. Prayer isn't optional, but rather an expectation of Heaven. Hearing these words pierced my heart as a believer. What I heard was that the father desired to speak with me and His expectation was that at some point I would *enter in.*

Prayer is a dimension of conversation we have with the father and it was Jesus' expectation of *all* His disciples to pray. When Jesus said, "But when you pray," he was correcting the errant prayers of the hypocrites. He was also letting His disciples know "I have another expectation of you and so does the Father". See, being heard in heaven isn't determined by the level, length, or eloquence of your voice; but in the posture of your heart and your desire to pursue time with Abba.

Prayer is "entering into," as the scripture says, "your most private room". Prayer is an intimate place and space where it's just you and daddy God, where you're able to breathe after you've handled all the business of the day and exhale into His arms. We've seemingly turned prayer into something laborious and that it not all there is to prayer. While travailing prayer may take labor, the pursuit of prayer, of any type, should not be laborious, but exciting. I recall a time where I was running errands with my father and I seemed to be a little anxious to complete the task at hand. My father and in a sarcastic tone said, "you act like you want to get rid of me," funny right? It wasn't that I wanted to get rid of him, but I was so hungering to spend time with Father God to exhale in His arms, to tell Him how much I loved Him, and hear Him say "I love you more".

Entering into prayer, requires you shut the door. Entering in, required me to come ready to shut the door on what was going on at that current moment, so I could embrace, with joy, what was to come in the encounter of His presence. See, growing up there were only a few "seasoned believers" who had a fervor for seeking the face of the Lord. I wasn't raised in a culture were there was an entire community of God lovers but rather a handful of women who loved to pursue the Father, in prayer, and they really believed in that. As a man, in the early stages of my early Christian walk, it was weird to be considered a prayer warrior. I've come to not only challenge that, but I've also come to bring truth that Jesus, as a man, had a very serious prayer life of "entering in".

Often times, you will find in scripture where Jesus left the crowd to go away into a mountain and pray. We have to be hungrier for the Father than we are for the acknowledgement or the title of "Intercessor" or "Prayer Warrior." While those are great aspirations, if they are not rooted in deep love with the Father, it's vain glory we seek. These are things I learned early in my prayer development stages.

Prayer isn't only entering into conversation, it is an expectation of Heaven. Prayer is the privilege and responsibility of the sons of God. Jesus taught His disciples "Pray to your Father". Wait a minute so you're telling me that prayer helps me identify God as Father? YES! It was in prayer that I began to see myself as a son of God and it was in prayer that He showed me my inheritance as His child. Growing up as a pastors kid, when I faced peer challenges in the ministry or even felt bullied by some of the leadership, my response was "I'm telling my dad." Why? Because I was confident in His ability to fix those situations. Likewise, entering into my prayer time I was able to "tell my dad" and I was fully confident that He was able to not only fix my situation but fix me *in* my situation. Prayer isn't just giving the Father access to fix your situation but to allow the Father to fix you in your situation. The chastening of the Father identifies me as a son of God.

Entering into prayer is amazing. Often times, I wonder why its the least attended gathering in most churches. It can be discouraging if you're focused on the number of bodies who show up at a prayer meeting. However, I've come to focus on Him showing up and as long as the father is present it really doesn't matter who isn't. I remember when I established corporate prayer gatherings into our assembly having written in my heart "My house shall be called a House of Prayer." I was not dishonorably stating this, but I was seeing everything else but that pulse of the House of God which was, is, and forever shall be prayer. The maximum number of attendees was about 10, and I learned to be faithful with those who came. The Lord used me to teach them lessons on prayer and how to get answered prayers. As a leader, seeing their hunger for biblical truth grow, concerning prayer, was fulfilling.

The reason this book is entitled the *Journal of an Intercessor* is because this journey in prayer is very real and very personal. I want to help and encourage developing intercessors to keep standing and keep dwelling in the shadow of the Almighty.

9 After this manner therefore pray ye: Our Father which art in heaven, Hallowed be thy name.

10 Thy kingdom come, Thy will be done in earth, as it is in heaven. Matthew 6:9-10

Jesus taught His disciples "After this manner therefore pray ye." Do you see the reality of sonship here? "Our Father" Prayer is speaking to and addressing your Father in heaven. But what does prayer accomplish? The kingdom of God, done in earth, as it is in Heaven. Let me let you in on a huge secret that's been revealed. Since this scripture was penned, Heaven can't come, in Earth, until we enter into prayer. See, once you renew your mind and understand that prayer isn't just a boring conversation with the air, but an actual expectation that Heaven awaits to hear, we'd be encouraged to enter into prayer more intentionally. We enter into prayer, so Heaven can crash into the earth with the power of the kingdom of God and the will of the Father. Once we understand this, we will be like I was while running errands with my father. This is great, but Heaven is waiting on me to come release the Kingdom of God in the earth. Prayer is entering into agreement with the Father so that the Father can release Heaven on earth through you.

2 PROPHESY TO THE WIND

Get up! She said it's time to war. Startled by this alarming statement, I awakened, and I rubbed my eyes to see what time it was 3:30 am, you could imagine my response to my mother's urgent plea for war in the spirit. This was an unusual occurrence being as though she never wakened me to pray with her before, but when there is a soul on the line it's worth it all. As I sat there, watching her roll in the floor and speak in tongues, I thought to myself "wow she's really going at it". I stood up and began to war with her. Not knowing exactly what to pray I was reminded of the scripture *"...for we know not what we should pray as we ought: but the Spirit itself maketh intercession for us..." Romans 8:26*

As I began to pray in the spirit, travail prayer began to pour out of me. Now we had two crazy people at 3:30am rolling and crying out for a soul - commanding the powers of darkness to let her go and release her to the Kingdom of God. I got up from the floor and began to pace back and forth asking Holy Spirit what's next? It's vital that while making intercession for something to ask, seek, knock on Holy Spirit for the battle plan in prayer. He knows the mind of God for all souls and He makes those plans known to them who will seek.

"Prophesy to the winds," He said. My response was "excuse me sir." He said it again, "Prophesy to the winds," He spoke strongly. Often times, in moments of intense battle we get so carried away in battle that we never step back and ask God for the battle plan on how to gain victory. It's my belief that God is not only raising up warriors, but He's raising up skillful warriors that have allowed God to teach their fingers to war and their hands to fight. To my surprise, this realm of prophetic decree was new to me and I want to share it with you. God was bringing me into the understanding that the anointing goes beyond just casting out devils, healing the sick and destroying bondages; but it had authority in the "Cosmic Realms" remembering what the disciples stated on the Ship "...Even the winds obey Him(*Mark 4:41*)." You have to recognize that you have the same DNA of Jesus Christ and the winds will obey you.

The prophet Ezekiel understood this authority all too well. He was placed, by the spirit of the Lord, in a valley of bones; basically, a grave yard. This valley was a memorial of where life once was. Sometimes assignments look impossible, but I believe if He places it before us we already have authority in it. It doesn't matter how gripped in sin or bondage or how tightly hell's grip is on a soul, Gods power and authority has been given to us over all the power of the enemy. Praying into impossible situations releases *Gods Possibility*! God asked Ezekiel a question "And he said unto me, Son of man, can these bones live?" When God asked the question, He was already confident in the answer – "Prophesy upon these bones." When we are engaged in a realm of prophetic decree, we have to understand that within that prophetic utterance is the grace to fulfill that word and insure its manifestation. As a New Testament believer, we must understand that prophesying, for us, is done by faith. Paul the Apostle taught "Prophesy according to the proportion of your faith." Faith filled words don't fall to the ground, they are energized by Holy Spirit.

When in engaging in spiritual battle it's wise to assess the situation. Like any skilled military army, there must be scouts sent to see what occupies the land. The gift of discerning of spirits is vital to victory in the spirit. Then He said unto me,

"Prophesy unto the wind, prophesy, son of man, and say to the wind, thus saith the Lord God; Come from the four winds O breath, and breathe upon these slain, that they might live. (Ezekiel 32:9) Let's look at the damage that was done. There was seemingly no hope, this was a lost cause; a once victorious army is now a grave yard of dead bones. But despite what it was, God still saw the victorious army emerging and they needed a fresh breath from God to awaken what was laying as dead. The particular soul my mother and I were interceding for was dead with rebellion, rejection, abandonment, and sexual sin. They looked pretty much like the dry bones. In the valley, sin dries you out and makes you emotionless to the things of God. After receiving wisdom from Holy Spirit on what to do, I prophesied as He commanded. Before we move further, I want to you to know that each wind carries a different meaning.

- **East Winds** – East winds can be winds of deliverance and breakthrough. In Exodus 14:15-16, it was a strong east wind that split the red sea and allowed Israel to cross over on dry ground. East winds (As Judgement) can also bring famine and drought. In Exodus 10:12-15, the east wind carried locusts which ate every herb of the land and all the fruit of the trees which the hail had left.

- **West Winds**- The west wind normally brings refreshing to what the east wind has brought. In Exodus 10:19, it was the west wind that took away the locusts and cast them into the sea. The west wind also carries rain and blows from the setting of the sun, revealing end of the day even reset and restoration.

- **North Winds**- Proverbs 25:23 reveals that the north wind brings the rain. Ezekiel 1:4 reveals that it carries wind storms and brightness. The North wind carries conviction, judgement, reproving and revival according to Jeremiah 51:6.

- **South Winds**- Luke 12:55 reveals the south winds can be hot. However, it can also bring peace, quietness and tranquility according to Acts 27:13.

Now that we have a clearer understanding of the winds and what they carry, we can better call forth the wind that carries what we need. Once again, this soul we were contending for had been dry with rebellion, sexual sin, hardships and rejection, and was just in a bad place. But also, in a place of ignoring God, she was in an east wind circumstance and needed a North West wind to hit her life. So, I prophesied as I was commanded.

"Oh, North West winds blow. Bring conviction, bring revival, bring healing and restoration. blow her back into her purpose, blow her back in love with Jesus, remove the heat and destructions of the east winds in her life in Jesus Name." and as I began to prophesy and command the winds within 20 minutes literally, breakthrough, for that individual came. Regardless of what the situation may look like, be like Ezekiel and prophesy life into dead situations.

3 UNDERSTANDING PRAYER PORTALS

As the "house of God" we must have a clear understanding and revelation that we are the "Gate of Heaven." We are the entry point to how heaven meets and contacts the Earth. We stand at the point where angels ascend and descend!

Genesis 28:10-19 (KJV)

10 And Jacob went out from Beersheba, and went toward Haran.

11 And he lighted upon a certain place, and tarried there all night, because the sun was set; and he took of the stones of that place, and put them for his pillows, and lay down in that place to sleep.

12 And he dreamed, and behold a ladder set up on the earth, and the top of it reached to heaven: and behold the angels of God ascending and descending on it.

13 And, behold, the Lord stood above it, and said, I am the Lord God of Abraham thy father, and the God of Isaac: the land whereon thou liest, to thee will I give it, and to thy seed;

14 And thy seed shall be as the dust of the earth, and thou shalt spread abroad to the west, and to the east, and to the north, and to the south: and in thee and in thy seed shall all the families of the earth be blessed.

15 And, behold, I am with thee, and will keep thee in all places whither thou goest, and will bring thee again into this land; for I will not leave thee, until I have done that which I have spoken to thee of.

16 And Jacob awaked out of his sleep, and he said, Surely the Lord is in this place; and I knew it not.

17 And he was afraid, and said, How dreadful is this place! this is none other but the house of God, and this is the gate of heaven.

18 And Jacob rose up early in the morning, and took the stone that he had put for his pillows, and set it up for a pillar, and poured oil upon the top of it.

19 And he called the name of that place Bethel: but the name of that city was called Luz at the first.

By this encounter we understand that there is a place by which heaven and earth connect and it's through the house of God or "Bethel". To understand the house of God, we must know what God defines as the House of God. From this, we see several indicators of the House of God:

• Open Heavens

• Prophetic Insight (Dreams Visions)

• Angelic Encounters

• Supernatural Encounters

• A place of Supply and Exchange (Ladder)

• Revealing and Unlocking Destiny and Inheritance

• The Voice of God

Bethel, "The House of God", was created for receiving and releasing the supply of heaven into the earth. But HOW? Notice in verse 18, Jacob took the stone and poured oil on in as an act of honor and named it. Places of encounters are worth remembering. The House of God should be a place of constant encounters. Jacob created an altar, a place where He encountered the Lord. However, it was because He was afraid. "Encounters should increase the fear of the Lord in our Hearts!" I believe it's the fear of God in our hearts that creates a passion and desire to experience more of God.

Isaiah 56:5-8 (KJV)

5 Even unto them will I give in mine house and within my walls a place and a name better than of sons and of daughters: I will give them an everlasting name, that shall not be cut off.

6 Also the sons of the stranger, that join themselves to the Lord, to serve him, and to love the name of the Lord, to be his servants, every one that keepeth the sabbath from polluting it, and taketh hold of my covenant;

7 Even them will I bring to my holy mountain, and make them joyful in my house of prayer: their burnt offerings and their sacrifices shall be accepted upon mine altar; for mine house shall be called an house of prayer for all people.

8 The Lord God, which gathereth the outcasts of Israel saith, Yet will I gather others to him, beside those that are gathered unto him.

After Jacob, in Genesis, talks about the supernatural access point of the House of God Isaiah shows how this takes place. He defines, if you will, for us what the House of God is - "For mine house shall be called an House of Prayer". It is prayer that allows for heavens supply to enter into the earth. Even Jesus

Christ taught "Thy Kingdom Come, Thy Will Be Done". It's all on the foundation of prayer and intercession. Prayer gives us access to "portals". The blessing of accessing a prayer portal is the fact that through that portal the supply of Heaven can enter into the earth without demonic interference. That's why Elijah was able to shut the heavens so there would be NO Rain but, in the turnaround, He prayed earnestly and there was a release of RAIN! It was prayer that opened the Heavens so that rain could come to supply the earth, crops, and the ground. From what God spoke to Isaiah concerning the house of God being the house of prayer, let's look at a few things He Promises:

- **Give them an Everlasting Name**

- **House for the Rejected (Spirit of Adoption)**

- **Fruitful Life**

- **Experience Joyfulness**

- **Come into covenant**

- **Acceptance (You've been accepted the beloved)**

- **Worship in Spirit and in Truth**

- **Intercession**

This is the culture of the house of prayer, the place where the Lord is Abba! Now that we understand that the house of God is the house of prayer let's look at the intercessors assignment concerning the house of prayer. There is something about intercession that arouses angelic response. We have, as intercessors, a responsibility to open and access prayer portals bringing this house into abundance and supply, but you must know that angels aid in the transit of supply.

Revelation 8:3-4 (AMPC)

3And another angel came and stood over the altar. He had a golden censer, and he was given very much incense (fragrant spices and gums which exhale perfume when burned), that he might mingle it with the prayers of all the people of God (the saints) upon the golden altar before the throne.

4 And the smoke of the incense (the perfume) arose in the presence of God, with the prayers of the people of God (the saints), from the hand of the angel.

We learn from this scripture that our prayers are gathered by angels and mixed with incense. So, angels are responding and gathering what we as intercessors and saints are praying and releasing. They have a responsibility to make sure our prayers get to the place of exchange, So, when they come back as manifestation, they are to match the blessing assigned by the Creators design and will.

The spiritual portal is the equivalent of all that the anointing can supply as a sign of God's approval and covenant provisions. Portals are also equivalent to windows of heaven (Genesis 7:11; 8:2) Through intercessory prayer, and other acts of spiritual protocols and righteousness, one opens and keeps open the portals of their life.

4 THE HEART OF THE INTERCESSOR

Guard your heart with all diligence for out of it flows the issues of life *(Proverbs 4:23)*. This is a very familiar scripture to any person who's been walking with the Lord for any extent of time, but very few really spend time intentionally guarding their heart. Let's look at how The Message translation states it "Keep vigilant watch over your heart; that's where life starts." If life starts with my heart I should take it more seriously, don't you think? If my heart is full of poison that means my life will be and could very well eventually lead to an early grave.

Guarding your heart is essential to all believers, especially those who have been deemed intercessors or prayer warriors. Keeping a clean heart in prayer ensures that the prayers you're praying aren't jaded by your own biased opinions. I know you're saying "Jonathan, well how do I keep a clean and guarded heart when there are constant blows in my life?" I'm glad you asked.

Luke 17:1-4 (KJV)

1Then said he unto the disciples, it is impossible but that offences will come: but woe unto him, through whom they come!

2 It were better for him that a millstone were hanged about his neck, and he cast into the sea, than that he should offend one of these little ones.

3 Take heed to yourselves: If thy brother trespass against thee, rebuke him; and if he repent, forgive him.

4 And if he trespass against thee seven times in a day, and seven times in a day turn again to thee, saying, I repent; thou shalt forgive him.

Jesus taught us something here. Our first lesson is that we must understand that "offense will come"! Let's get rid of that erroneous mindset that we are the only ones that get offended. What we should learn is how to deal with offenses when they do show up. Jesus lays out the perfect blueprint for us here in Luke "take heed to yourselves." Do you mean that even if I'm innocent in the situation, I still have to handle it? YES! Family, we must understand that offenses can come from all directions, from the most random people, and in the most random of situations.

I remember, one time, while driving to the hospital to go visit my sister, my mom just decided that I had a speed demon and decided to address it. Long story short, we got into a brief intense fellowship until I heard Holy Spirit speak to me and say, "it's not what it seems". At that moment, I ended the fellowship and casted off the spirit of offense. After all, I was going into the hospital to pray for the sick.

Offense comes to ensnare our heart so the power of Holy Spirit is blocked up. Offenses are designed to hit our heart and that's where life is. Jesus said, "rebuke him," meaning handle it, address the offense, and then forgive. We can no longer go on in life without dealing with our offense. When we do, we become like professional dysfunctional, but functional alcoholics. The only difference is we're not intoxicated with wine but offense after offense.

"Forgive Him!" What a bold statement Jesus says. He doesn't exactly give us a choice, but He boldly states "forgive him". How many of us have made the statement "I'll forgive, but I won't forget"? Forgetting is synonymous to forgiveness. Forgiving is a freewill act of the heart (where life starts). After all, Jesus forgave you. The moment we begin to defend our right to be offended, we invite bitterness and then sickness, however that's a different lesson for a different day. Forgiveness is vital to answered prayer.

Matthew 6:15 (KJV)

15 But if ye forgive not men their trespasses, neither will your Father forgive your trespasses.

Jesus was teaching His disciples upon request to pray after laying out the model prayer we call the "Lord's Prayer" He responds by saying "For if ye forgive men" Jesus connected the ministry of prayer to the power of forgiveness. See the heart of the intercessor must be one free of offenses and full of forgiveness. The ministry of intercession is full of mercy and mercy hinges on forgiveness.

Mark 11:23-26 (KJV)

23 For verily I say unto you, That whosoever shall say unto this mountain, Be thou removed, and be thou cast into the sea; and shall not doubt in his heart, but shall believe that those things which he saith shall come to pass; he shall have whatsoever he saith.

24 Therefore I say unto you, What things soever ye desire, when ye pray, believe that ye receive them, and ye shall have them.

25 And when ye stand praying, forgive, if ye have ought against any: that your Father also which is in heaven may forgive you your trespasses.

26 But if ye do not forgive, neither will your Father which is in heaven forgive your trespasses.

It's interesting to me that Jesus would connect answered prayer to the heart postures of the petitioner. Often times in scripture Jesus rebuked His disciples for their hard heart do the doubt and unbelief. Here Jesus speaks of the removal of mountains being connected to the heart of the petitioner being full of Faith.

5 PROPHETIC INTERCESSION

John 13:25 (KJV)

He then lying on Jesus' breast saith unto him, Lord, who is it?

The posture of prophetic intercession is like John the beloved, leaning into the heart of Jesus and inquiring of Him. "Lord, who is it?" is a powerful statement, but often it is overlooked. I personally believe the reason John could ask such a bold statement is because He was leaning into the heart of Jesus. Those who will be bold enough to lay their heads on Jesus' bosom have authority to ask, "Lord, who is it?" This is the posture of prophetic intercession - being intimate enough to pray beyond your own prayer list to receive the heart of Jesus and press into it. Often times, in prayer, we never tap into the place of prophetic intercession because we're so consumed with our own selfish prayer lists and desires, that we forget that Jesus sits as King over an entire world.

My first encounter in this realm of prayer was in 2006. I believe I was cleaning my bathroom and I began to weep and cry and speak to God about being overwhelmed and tired of what I was dealing with at that moment. I was telling him how I just couldn't go on and I needed a break, or I would break. Then, I began to pray in the spirit and I saw my music teachers' face and I knew then my petitions weren't the cries of my heart, but of hers. What I learned about intercession early is that as intercessors we don't just pray *for* someone we pray *as* someone. I was sensitive enough to tap into the soul cry of a lady whom I'd never known outside of choir practice.

Being led by Holy Spirit is vital to the breakthroughs acquired in prophetic intercession. That next day, I was walking to lunch and Holy Spirit said to me "Jonathan, go share this encounter with her." I thought to myself "God she will think I'm a crazy kid." What I didn't know was, God was training me to trust the voice of Holy Spirit. Nervously, but obediently, I went and shared, and her response blew me away. She said, "Jon that was Holy Spirit. Last night around that time I was telling my husband those exact words." This is what I adore about prophetic intercession. It carries so much of the heart of Jesus that while folks are weary and tired, Jesus breathes upon our prayer womb to intercept, intervene, and interpose His goodness on their behalf.

Being sensitive and available to Holy spirit and his calling you into a deeper place of intercession, is a must. The invitation to more, is the invitation to laying on the bosom of Jesus. I was attending a mens conference in Indiana and during worship there was a father and son in front of me. During the entire time of worship the son kept laying his head on His father's shoulder and the Father kept kissing the forehead of his son and Holy Spirit said to me, "Jonathan those who will lean into my bosom will be kissed by my presence and glory." This is His heart behind prophetic intercession. The goal is to be kissed by Him, to carry His mark upon us so when we pray His heart is revealed and released. Who would have thought that a simple father and son relationship could speak so profoundly about prophetic intercession?

You're reading this book because you've had encounters that you couldn't explain, or you're feeling the deeper call and pull into another place in your prayer life. I've learned that it's those who won't ignore those little prompts to pray, that God shares

His heart with. The irony of such a statement is that He desires to share with all His children, but the reality is all His children won't pay the price to lay on His bosom. John the beloved was able to write the book of "Revelation", which is the Revelation of Jesus Christ, because He was willing to do what the disciples didn't and that was lay on Jesus' bosom. He carried the mysteries of days he hadn't yet seen. When we make that sacrifice, eternity opens up to us in ways and realms we haven't known. Are you willing to pay the price of becoming a beloved one?

Have you ever gone into your prayer closet and nothing happened, you felt empty and void like Jesus where are you? Those moments that make you say, "I'm here where are you?" Great! Then you will appreciate what I'm about to say. This revelation came to me after time spent asking those "God I'm here, where are you?" questions. This is a major key to *effective* prophetic intercession it's called "waiting on the Lord". Waiting on the Lord in prayer is apart of the posture of leaning your head into his bosom to hear the rhythm of His beating heart.

Psalm 130:5-6 (KJV)

5 I wait for the Lord, my soul doth wait, and in his word do I hope.

6 My soul waiteth for the Lord more than they that watch for the morning: I say, more than they that watch for the morning.

Waiting on the Lord opens us up to visions and encounters. David was so serious about waiting on the Lord that he said, "I wait for you more than they that watch for the morning." Where is your expectation? When He becomes our expectation, we won't mind waiting before the Lord. Waiting is for the hungry and expectant. Sometimes, it's in vision that the heart of God is revealed to us and we are to pray into them, ultimately releasing His heart. God's heart always has His will attached to it. He's looking for someone in the earth to agree with His heart, so His will can be manifested in the earth.

Habakkuk 2:1 (KJV)

I will stand upon my watch, and set me upon the tower, and will watch to see what he will say unto me, and what I shall answer when I am reproved.

Habakkuk was on to something here and I want us to see that watching is synonymous to waiting. When he said, "and will watch to see what He will say unto me", he was showing us that leaning into His heart opens you up to prophetic visions.

A classic practice taken from this topic of prophetic intercession, is Daniels 21-day pursuit for the deliverance of His nation. One mans obedience to pray, set his nation free, but not without a fight. Let's look at little closer to His story and help you understand some guidelines and things to expect praying into the dimension of prophetic intercession. Daniel was one who had a constant prayer life. He was devoted to God and refused to bow down to anti-God systems and worship. Daniel had compassion for his nation and I believe his compassion was birthed out of the place of prayer he built, over the years, with the Father.

There are some classic principles that will help you enter into the dimension of prophetic intercession.

1. Awareness:
Daniel 9:1-2 (KJV)

1 In the first year of Darius the son of Ahasuerus, of the seed of the Medes, which

was made king over the realm of the Chaldeans;

2 In the first year of his reign I Daniel understood by books the number of the years, whereof the word of the Lord came to Jeremiah the prophet, that he would accomplish seventy years in the desolations of Jerusalem.

It was Daniels awareness of the prophetic word, spoken by Jeremiah the prophet, that even awakened him to press into heaven for his nation. Sometimes we have to recall prophetic words spoken over ourselves, our families, ministries, states, and nations and begin to engage heaven with that word. Awareness brings us into spiritual sensitivity. Begin to ask Holy Spirit to give you a greater awareness and bring back the prophetic words spoken over you.

2. Revelation
Daniel 9:21-22 (KJV)

21 Yea, whiles I was speaking in prayer, even the man Gabriel, whom I had seen in the vision at the beginning, being caused to fly swiftly, touched me about the time of the evening oblation.

22 And he informed me, and talked with me, and said, O Daniel, I am now come forth to give thee skill and understanding.

Revelation is a huge part of prophetic intercession. It takes revelation to see into the realm of the spirit and pick up the heartbeat of heaven, as it pertains to the petition. Gabriel came to impart skill and understanding which came from heaven, nothing of this earth. When engaging prophetic intercession, one must be willing to allow Holy Spirit to breathe on their understanding.

3. Angels
Daniel 10:9-12 (KJV)

9 Yet heard I the voice of his words: and when I heard the voice of his words, then

was I in a deep sleep on my face, and my face toward the ground.

10 And, behold, an hand touched me, which set me upon my knees and upon the palms of my hands.

11 And he said unto me, O Daniel, a man greatly beloved, understand the words that I speak unto thee, and stand upright: for unto thee am I now sent. And when he had spoken this word unto me, I stood trembling.

12 Then said he unto me, Fear not, Daniel: for from the first day that thou didst set thine heart to understand, and to chasten thyself before thy God, thy words were heard, and I am come for thy words.

Revelation 8:4 (KJV)

4 And the smoke of the incense, which came with the prayers of the saints, ascended up before God out of the angel's hand.

Angels are a huge part of prophetic intercession. They come and bring help in the realm of the spirit. There is something about intercession that stirs angelic response. Angels are helps ministers that have been assigned to aid us as believers. The angelic assistance that Daniel received, as a result of prophetic intercession, brought him and the nation into breakthrough!

4. Breakthrough
Daniel 10:20-21 (KJV)

20 Then said he, Knowest thou wherefore I come unto thee? and now will I return

to fight with the prince of Persia: and when I am gone forth, lo, the prince of Grecia shall come.

21 But I will shew thee that which is noted in the scripture of truth: and there is none that holdeth with me in these things, but Michael your prince.

The ultimate goal of all intercession, especially prophetic intercession, is breakthrough! We want to see the power of God heal, save, deliver, and set free!

Prophetic intercession begins to bring divine reset over nations. Daniel was resisted by a Prince of Persia, which was the demonic hold over the nation. It took Daniels' intercession, mixed with revelation, fasting, and angelic assistance to unseat that Dark Prince from withholding breakthrough over that nation.

6 MY PRAYER LIFE DID THIS

The intercessors warfare doesn't have as much to do with the demonic, as it does with the soul of the intercessor. Your soul is comprised of three parts:

1. **Will**

2. **Mind**

3. **Emotions**

What I've discovered during my time as one given to prayer is that a lot of what I've experienced was only to wrought compassion in me. So, when I stand in the gap I'm standing with the feeling of the person, city, nation I'm standing for. The whole idea is to become Christ-compatible because He was touched with the feelings of our infirmities. In that same manner, the warfare the intercessor encounters builds, within them, the ability to intercede from a place of understanding, revelation, and experience. Sometimes, if we're not discerning, we will think the attack is because we failed God; but really, it's because we've been so committed to Him in building a life of prayer!

The great part about the intercessors' warfare is the reward is so full of glory that it makes the warfare worth it. Let's take a look at the life of Daniel. He was clearly a man dedicated to building a consistent life of prayer. The truth of the matter is Daniel wasn't tossed into the lions' den because He failed God or because He fell into sin. However, it was his relentless pursuit of God and His presence that nominated Daniel for the lions' den. What amazed me the most about Daniel's story is that scripture tells us in

Daniel 6:10(KJV)

Now when Daniel knew that the writing was signed, he went into his house; and his windows being open in his chamber toward Jerusalem, he kneeled upon his knees three times a day, and prayed, and gave thanks before his God, as he did aforetime.

Daniel had knowledge of the decree and the fact that the King signed it, but that didn't stop his pursuit. He continued to pursue, wholly, as was his custom. What really ministers to me is the fact that Daniel was so faithful to God the enemy couldn't find anything to slander him. Since he could not slander Daniel, he created a law to ensnare Daniel. Let me prophesy to you quickly and encourage you that your season of warfare isn't because God is mad at you, but because you're so faithful to Him - your prayer life did this. It was prayer that got you here and it's prayer that's going to get you out! Intercessors never become so overwhelmed in the heat of battle that you lose focus of the truth and the truth is found in

Psalm 34:19(KJV)

Many are the afflictions of the righteous: but the Lord delivereth him out of them all.

The truth of this matter is "The Lord delivereth"; declare that with me now.

THE LORD DELIVERETH! YES! The very king who signed the decree that was crafted for Daniels' death was the same king that couldn't sleep until Daniel was released.

Daniel 6:16-20 (KJV)

16 Then the king commanded, and they brought Daniel, and cast him into the den of lions. Now the king spake and said unto Daniel, Thy God whom thou servest continually, he will deliver thee.

17 And a stone was brought, and laid upon the mouth of the den; and the king sealed it with his own signet, and with the signet of his lords; that the purpose might not be changed concerning Daniel.

18 Then the king went to his palace, and passed the night fasting: neither were instruments of musick brought before him: and his sleep went from him.

19 Then the king arose very early in the morning, and went in haste unto the den of lions.

20 And when he came to the den, he cried with a lamentable voice unto Daniel: and the king spake and said to Daniel, O Daniel, servant of the living God, is thy God, whom thou servest continually, able to deliver thee from the lions?

This entire plot was to stop Daniels "free will" to pray to the Most High God. The warfare we encounter is designed to keep us from being "willing" to pray or make intercession in behalf of our family, city, states, and nations. When we ask God to increase our prayer life, He doesn't send us a manuscript He sends the fire. Learning how to pray beyond the emotion of what you're currently facing can only come by doing exactly that - praying through. This is what Jesus did when he was in the garden praying "Father remove this cup." Scripture says, He prayed so fervently that his sweat was like drops of blood, however after He prayed angels came and strengthened Him. The objective is to pray beyond...until you come into strength for the next assignment.

7 PRAYING WITH THE WORD

It's very important that we learn as prayer warriors, intercessors, and prayer leaders to pray the word of God. In my travels and in my experience, prayer meeting can get really whacky when the word isn't present. Praying the word guarantees results as long as we're led by Holy Spirit. I think much of our frustration with prayer is that we've been taught to pray without Holy Spirit leading.

We often confuse our presumption for faith in God. When we don't see our desired results, we either blame Satan or we feel as though we didn't have enough faith. Most times, it's neither; it's just a lack of being led by Holy Spirit. This is where I believe a lot of us get off track or draw back in prayer. We allow the enemy to lie and say things like "See this prayer thing doesn't work" or "You'll never have enough faith. You should just stop," those are all lies that need to be cast down from its high place.

The truth of the matter is, most of us haven't been taught how to allow Holy Spirit to lead us in prayer. Now I'm not saying I have anything against prayer lists and prayer targets, but sometimes it's ok to come to God with faith believing that He is. Sometimes our prayer targets aren't what Holy Spirit desires to press into at the current prayer time. Those who are led by the spirit are called the sons of God. We

have to learn to yield to the leading of Holy Spirit, even in prayer. After all He knows the mind of God, and who better to lead us than Holy Spirit.

John 1:1-3 (AMPC)

1 In the beginning [before all time] was the Word (Christ), and the Word was with God, and the Word was God Himself.

2 He was present originally with God.

3 All things were made and came into existence through Him; and without Him was not even one thing made that has come into being.

If we take a close look at the book of John, in the first chapter, we see that the Genesis of creation started with the Word whom we know is Jesus. He was the embodiment of prophecy and scripture fulfilled. If it started with the Word, it has to be sustained with and by the Word. So, having your spirit full of the word, which I like to call spirit food, is when Holy Spirit prompts us to prayer or leads us in what to pray. He's going to cause the Word in our belly to come forth and that is called "The Sword of the Spirit".

The word becomes a weapon when we allow Holy Spirit to breathe on it. Holy Spirit inspired prayer always gets heavens results. It's one thing to loosely quote scripture out of presumption, but it's another to allow Holy Spirit to bring up out of your spirit His word and you use it skillfully in prayer. I remember back in 2014, we were preparing to go to Florida for a prophetic conference and I had no money to put towards purchasing my plane ticket or hotel. I did not even have the money to pay the $200.00 registration fee. I had a conversation with my spiritual mom and she said, "Jon, how dare you have faith to believe God to get people out of wheel chairs; but not believe Him for finances?" That sharp rebuke didn't feel good to my flesh at all.

I had to take a step back and begin to repent for my limited thinking concerning God's provisions. You know how I got that trip financed? You guessed it! I had to pray the word, but I wasn't loosely quoting scriptures on Gods provisions and promises, I asked Holy Spirit what is the word I need to stand on for this trip to Florida? Waiting on Him was key. Beloved, waiting on the Lord renews and strengthens your faith in Him.

Isaiah 40:31(AMPC)

But those who wait for the Lord [who expect, look for, and hope in Him] shall change and renew their strength and power; they shall lift their wings and mount up [close to God] as eagles [mount up to the sun]; they shall run and not be weary, they shall walk and not faint or become tired.

The more I waited on Him the stronger I became, and I heard him say "I shall supply", so I went further in the word.

Philippians 4:19(AMPC)

And my God will liberally supply (fill to the full) your every need according to His riches in glory in Christ Jesus.

I began to use the word as a sword to cut down doubt and unbelief in my heart and declare "God you shall supply"! You know, I sense you who are reading this need to declare that "My God, you shall supply" - make it personal. Don't you know I received over what I needed and even had some left over to purchase new luggage! When you wait on Holy Spirit to breathe upon the word you will get results.

1 John 5:14(AMPC)

And this is the confidence (the assurance, the privilege of boldness) which we have in Him: [we are sure] that if we ask anything (make any request) according to His will (in agreement with His own plan), He listens to and hears us.

Confidence in prayer comes from knowing He hears us. How do we know He hears us? We've asked according to His will. This is why it is of vital importance to allow Holy Spirit to lead us in prayer. He will always lead us into the perfect will of God. Holy Spirit is required to actualize the word of God. He's heavens administrator, making sure the word of God accomplishes and performs all that it's designed to do.

As I stated earlier, the sword of the spirit is the word of God. Paul the Apostle, by the will of God, lets us know in Ephesians that the word of God is apart of our spiritual armor. It is needed for us to wage effective warfare and be victorious in this life. His word is the sword of the sprit and is sharper than any two-edged sword. As previously stated, when Holy Spirit brings up the word of God that's been stored down in you, it becomes the sword of the spirit. Why? I'm glad you asked! When faced with circumstances beyond your control, you need God's governing word to cut through barriers that have been set up by the enemy to delay Gods purpose in your life.

Remember, Holy Spirit defends the counsel of the Godhead and insures His purposes in our lives. When that purpose is threatened to be infiltrated by antichrist armies, heavens power source intervenes wielding the sword of the spirit, which is the word of God. You will find yourself in a realm of prayer and intercession where you are making declarations and decrees and that word is a sword piercing and cutting through the darkness that would try and bring confusion to the plans of God in your life. The sword of the spirit can also be used in praying for healing, commanding the sword to cut way tumors and growths in the bodies of our loved ones. It is written, "He sent His word (Jesus) to heal them". When I was ordained as an Elder, one of the ordination counselors stated to me something that has stuck with me forever. She said, "Jonathan the word of God is the final authority in every situation," and I leave those same words with you. *The word of God is the final authority in every situation!*

8 THE GATES OF PRAISE

Growing up in a traditional, however, charismatic Baptist and Pentecostal environment; including worship as a part of intercession wasn't the norm or so I thought. But now that I think about it we often opened up prayer meeting with a hymn of some sort but didn't give much attention to it. It wasn't until later in my years of being developed as an intercessor that I began to marry the two - worship and intercession. This revelation brought such a revolutionary change in my time with the Lord. The foundation of this revelation came weirdly to me, but I believe it was the divine timing of the Father, because He knows when we can handle the next level of truth and be made free.

I was laying on my mothers' bed and I came across a teaching that opened my eyes to a new realm of prayer I hadn't known - the work of worship and intercession Prior to receiving this radical message, I never thought that worship was just as important as my intercession with words. In fact, I learned that worship was intercession as well and that I could war with the song of the Lord and I could sing over situations, people, and nations.

Hosea 10:11-12

11 And Ephraim is as an heifer that is taught, and loveth to tread out the corn; but I passed over upon her fair neck: I will make Ephraim to ride; Judah shall plow, and Jacob shall break his clods.

12 Sow to yourselves in righteousness, reap in mercy; break up your fallow ground: for it is time to seek the Lord, till he come and rain righteousness upon you.

The scriptures above radically transformed my prayer life forever. The key statements here are "Judah shall plow", and "Jacob shall break his clods". Judah comes from the Hebrew word "yada" meaning to:

- shoot

- cast

- throw

- give thanks

We have to come into this understanding that when I'm worshipping, I'm shooting forth the presence and power of God over every bondage that would hold souls captive. When we worship we are literally throwing down the high places Satan has set up. However, there is something I want us to really understand that Hosea states here, "Judah shall plow". The action of plowing is great imagery and it shows me that my worship causes things to be loosened and released. Much like those who have a green thumb, they plow the ground to get ready for planting season. When we worship, when we "yada" over nations, situations, and souls we're preparing them to receive deliverance, breakthrough, and redemption. Praise and worship is as powerful as declarations and decrees because it is just that, a decree set to music.

Isaiah spoke prophetically that the house of God would be known internationally as the house of prayer for all people. One major lesson Holy Spirit taught me is that praise wasn't just a weapon, but it was also a gate. It was a place of entry and transition where we enter from one realm into another - a place of connection and release.

Isaiah 60:18 (KJV)

18 Violence shall no more be heard in thy land, wasting nor destruction within thy borders; but thou shalt call thy walls Salvation, and thy gates Praise.

Praise, as a gateway, brings us into a fresh perspective of the dynamics of praise. When we come into the revelation that praise is a gate, we take on a new sense of responsibility that before I enter into intercession I must first establish the entry point of praise allowing others to come into and through that gate.

9 THEREFORE COME

One of the most powerful revelations I received as an intercessor was in some of my most painful seasons. Every season reveals a fresh perspective of God. I remember a Sunday morning during worship there was such a strong reverence for God that overtook me. I felt Him calling me to the altar and as I walked up and knelt down with bitter tears streaming down my face, I heard him say "Jonathan (as He paused) I'm big enough to handle your brokenness". The tears ran increasingly down my face, but they turned from bitter tears to tears of joy and relief. At that moment, my spirit grew in faith because of the Father's word to me. When we come to Him we must approach Him not only in faith, but in the revelation we have of Him. Faith is honestly rooted in revelation. Without current revelation our faith will be weak.

As a believer called to prayer, it is very encouraging to know that Jesus was a man tempted; however, he never yielded to temptation. He was tested like we are but came out with victory which gives us hope of victory. Seasons come, and seasons go, but the word of the Lord remains the same; He never changes. This is the beautiful thing about Him. This is important to the intercessor because with every new revelation of Him revealed, we have the ability to establish that in an atmosphere. Prayer brings us into the understanding of the "Bigness" of our Father. Prayer reveals His might to us.

Hebrews 4:14-16 (KJV)

14 Seeing then that we have a great high priest, that is passed into the heavens, Jesus the Son of God, let us hold fast our profession.

15 For we have not an high priest which cannot be touched with the feeling of our infirmities; but was in all points tempted like as we are, yet without sin.

16 Let us therefore come boldly unto the throne of grace, that we may obtain mercy, and find grace to help in time of need.

The invitation to "Therefore Come" is based on the revelation of Him being "touched with my feelings". How confident does this truth make you? The momentum behind my pursuit is how real Jesus becomes to me. I'm able to boldly stand in His presence because He boldly revealed Himself to me. Prayer has a way of making God tangible. He becomes more than a Sunday school lesson or my preachers' sermon; He becomes my life source, my reason for being. This is vital to the intercessors faith. It was in that moment when the Father spoke to me, "Jonathan I'm big enough to handle your brokenness" that my Faith shot through the roof. Why? I began to understand that my life was an interest to Him, not just my call. Praying from this foundation makes prayer a privilege and not a duty.

Jesus' role as our High Priest offers us and invitation to "Boldly Come". The only way we can enter in is Jesus. Because of His sacrifice, once and for all, we have the confidence to enter therefore. Prayer requires movement. Entering into the throne requires me to move from natural realms into spiritual realms. Jesus, our High Priest, passed into the Heavens. This truth lets us know that were designed to pray from Heaven to Earth, not from Earth to Heaven.

Increasing my faith wasn't something that was easy when the Lord first began to develop my intercessory call. Being born and raised in a Christian family with pastors for parents, faith was normal. Even though faith was the norm, somewhere along the way I developed a mindset that the Father was only concerned about my spiritual walk, not the fullness of my life. Growing up, there was a song we sang often in our congregation and some of the lyrics say, "Oh what peace we often forfeit, oh what needless pains we bear, all because we do not carry everything to God in prayer". It wasn't until my early adult years I came into the fullness of that knowledge that Father cares for my life and not just my service. Entering in boldly into the throne room gives me the understanding that I have a right to come. When the accuser of the brethren tries to shoot forth his lies into our minds, we must cast those voices down and enter in because the blood of Jesus Christ made it possible.

Developing this mindset comes from understanding the sufficiency of Grace. It's our very weakest moments where He's made strong in us.

1 Peter 5:7 (KJV)

7 Casting all your care upon him; for he careth for you.

Casting our cares isn't always the easy thing to do, especially when you're used to being strong for everyone else. This is something I had to learn through bitter tears and trials. As an intercessor, my first level of prayer was "How could God allow me to intercede for other people, and nations, and I not know how to put on His strength"? That's exactly how He taught me to come boldly! He wanted me to bring Him everything, and when I say everything I mean everything. If I couldn't tell Jesus, who else could possibly help me?

Intercessor, you must learn to enter in boldly and press beyond the limitations that your religious barriers have taught you. You know we're very much like Adam, who allowed shame to hide him from the brightness of God's presence. Father is asking you, like He did Adam, "Intercessor, where are you? Why aren't you boldly coming to speak with me?" Coming into the truth that He cares for me gives me confidence to therefore boldly come.

10 PRAYING FOR BACKSLIDDEN LOVED ONES

I heard a minister say once at the close of His message, "if you're backslidden, all you need to do is slide back". I laughed when I heard it because, truth be told, sometimes it's that easy and other times it's not. The forces that helped you slide out of relationship with the Father are the same forces that keep souls in that state, and this is why intercession is Important. It's never the Fathers will that any man should perish. Dealing with stubborn devils requires much more force than a simple prayer at the altar. It often requires warring over the soul and involves prayers of binding and loosing. There is a war going on and we as believers must not be ignorant of Satan's devices.

Recently, I was asked to pray for someone very dear to my heart. Can I say that when someone asks for you to agree, in prayer, with them over a matter it's best to pray and not make void promises. Prayer causes the hand of God to deal with the hearts of men. If we don't pray, God can't intervene, and His kingdom can't come, and His will won't be done. The only way the will and kingdom of God can come in the earth is through praying people. After all, God himself sought for a man who would stand in the gap and make up the hedge(***Ezekiel 22:30***), and we must learn the seriousness of this kind of prayer because it saves lives.

When praying for backslidden loved ones, Holy Spirit has given me a great prayer strategy that brings breakthrough and deliverance. Depending on Holy Spirit is very key to breakthrough because He carries the mind of God. To see breakthrough, my intercession must sound like the mind of God. One of the words for intercession is "paga" which literally means, to strike and reach the mark. To be effective in my intercession, I must reach my target in the spirit I must shoot for the arrow of the Lords deliverance and hit the bullseye.

1. Agreement

Matthew 18:19 (KJV)

19 Again I say unto you, That if two of you shall agree on earth as touching any thing that they shall ask, it shall be done for them of my Father which is in heaven.

Praying the prayer of agreement is very important. Releasing your faith for someone else is a very powerful weapon against the bondages the enemy tries to ensnare the souls of man with. We cannot agree upon what we do not know about. Silent prayer requests are just as good as no prayer requests in my book. Touching requires something tangible, even our faith.

2. Insight

Jeremiah 29:11 (KJV)

11 For I know the thoughts that I think toward you, saith the Lord, thoughts of peace, and not of evil, to give you an expected end.

Insight is key in praying for the backslidden soul. God has a glorious plan for His children and that's the very thing Satan desires to abort. You must pray into Gods plan for the soul you're interceding for. Once you get a prophetic blueprint, you can war with that in the realm of the spirit by decreeing Gods destiny over their life.

3. Covenant

Jeremiah 3:14 (KJV)

14 Turn, O backsliding children, saith the Lord; for I am married unto you: and I will take you one of a city, and two of a family, and I will bring you to Zion:

Freedom is the covenant right of every believer even the backslidden. I remember holding my bible up to heaven and declaring God you're married to the backslider and you promised to bring them into Zion. I began to apply pressure to Gods delivering power by giving Him back His word of covenant.

4. Praise

Psalm 149:6 (KJV)

6 Let the high praises of God be in their mouth, and a two-edged sword in their hand;

The praise of God over a situation begins to shatter the chains of Hell. Many would call this intercessory praise. I just call it breakthrough Praise. Praise brings the anointing and the anointing destroys the yoke.

The more you learn to use the weapon of praise, the more insight you will receive on the power it brings forth. Praise confuses the camps of the enemy and they fall on their own weapons. Praise causes weapons formed against us, not to prosper.

5. Travailing Prayer

Isaiah 66:8 (KJV)

8 Who hath heard such a thing? who hath seen such things? Shall the earth be made to bring forth in one day? or shall a nation be born at once? for as soon as Zion travailed, she brought forth her children.

Travailing prayer is a realm of spirit-led, birthing that leads to birthing Gods promises in the earth. Travailing prayer involves weepings, tears, praying in the spirit and agonizing groans of the spirit. Travail in itself is the pain of child labor.

Romans 8:26 (KJV)

26 Likewise the Spirit also helpeth our infirmities: for we know not what we should pray for as we ought: but the Spirit itself maketh intercession for us with groanings which cannot be uttered.

Praying in the spirit leads us into travailing prayer. Praying, in the spirit, is a mighty weapon against hell's plot formed against our loved ones. When we give ourselves to the intercession of the spirit, we lead ourselves and others into supernatural breakthrough. Holy Spirit will always pray us into the mind of God. When we make intercession for our loved ones, by way of the spirit, we will bring them into Gods mind for their lives and ultimately bring them into the surrender to His will and plan for their life.

Made in the USA
Middletown, DE
06 August 2023